Things I Could Never Tell My Mother

(And Some Things She Told Me)

Drew Sheldon

This is a work of non-fiction. No names were
changed because no names were used.

Library of Congress Cataloging-in-Publication
Data is available upon request.

ISBN 978-1-7334244-0-0

Design and formatting by Drew Sheldon

For my mom, who for stylistic reasons is referred to as my mother in these pages, who always encouraged me to pursue my dreams, who gave me the antique manual typewriter upon which I learned to type, and who would be awfully proud of me for publishing this even though I would never let her read it.

Table of Contents

Part the Third: Addiction and Stuff

- Turn the Other Way
- Falling in Love with Booze
- Jumping Back into the Fire Water
- I've Got Calling Cards

Part the Fourth: Who's Afraid of Virginia Woolf?

- Sex, Lies, and Sexuality
- Which Will
- Roller Coaster of Love
- The First Time
- Jealous Girl
- Sounds and Silence

Part the Fifth: This Army Life

- Enlistment Blues
- Reasons Why
- Let's Have a Round for This Soldier
- Let's Have a Round for These Friends of Mine
- Let's Have Another Round

Part the Sixth: Post-Army Life and Career

- Give Them Shelter
- Lying Ears
- Home Again
- My Bridge Over Troubled Water

Part the Seventh: Some (Mostly) Happy Things

- My Blue-Eyed Girl
- I Need a Place to Hide Away
- Well, Actually…
- Who's the Lucky Guy?
- And So It Goes…

Introduction

First, I should mention that this is a trauma-focused memoir. This is by no means comprehensive. Some important people in my life are barely mentioned, and many more are not mentioned at all. Much of this space is taken by people who are no longer a part of my life, and very little is taken by people who are.

I wrote this in large part to purge myself of the pain these memories carry. I hope somehow it can help you do the same.

I have started and stopped this book multiple times. Much of it was written in the fall of 2015 with a couple things written in the winter of 2017/18. I started to do a full rewrite in the spring of 2019 but quickly abandoned that when I started reading all this other crap that I had already written. I figured it would be more fun to add, edit, and re-arrange things.

(Also, I'm lazy, and this is much easier.)

On that last parenthetical point, I should also mention that I decided to do this thing completely by myself. There are no editors, no beta readers, no nothing but me and my memories. So this might not be so good, but I realized I could never do it in the first place if I had to let people read it before I tried to publish it.

I must warn you that I cover a lot of heavy topics including death, suicide, war, sexual assault, various forms of abuse, and probably some other things that are not springing to mind right now. I included content warnings with each piece, but there is the possibility I missed something. So take care of yourself while you're reading this. It might not be easy. It definitely wasn't always easy to live.

Time Will Tell You

I tend to jump around in time when telling these tales. Things are arranged by overarching topics rather than in a linear fashion. So to help you navigate the temporal confusion, here is a timeline of some of the major events covered:

- March 1974: I was born in Michigan.
- Early 1984: I moved to the town where I would graduate high school.
- Summer 1990: My mom adopted my oldest nephew.
- Summer 2002: I quit drinking for the first time and got into a longtime relationship that I wrote about way too much.
- Fall 2002: I started volunteering at a crisis center.
- February 2007: I enlisted in the U.S. Army.
- July 2008: My father died.

- Early September 2008 — Late August 2009: Iraq.
- January 2011 — January 2012: Afghanistan.
- April 2011: My mom died.
- December 2012: I took my terminal leave from the U.S. Army and headed back to the Mitten.
- March 2013: I started working at a youth shelter.
- December 2013: I adopted a kitty named Francesca who drives me insane.
- December 2015: I start talking to a nice lady who would make me leave the Mitten again.
- September 2016: I started working at a group home.
- December 2017: I started working in a domestic violence intervention program.
- July 2018: I got married and had a hit song about a knife.
- (That last part is a private joke that you probably wouldn't enjoy that much anyway, but I assure you it is quite funny to a couple of us.)

Things My Mother
Told Me

Second Hand News

Content Warning: Death

"Hey Andrew, did you hear the news?"

My mother always called me by my full name. She loved to tell stories of how I insisted on it. Maybe it was because I knew she liked the name and that she would dislike me being called "Andy". Maybe it was one of my few rebellions. Most kids my age went by "Andy". I went by Andrew almost always until adulthood.

I didn't actually choose to shorten my name myself. I had a few friends who enjoyed shortening it, and since I wasn't having "Andy", they just lopped off that first syllable. And so "Drew" was born.

My mother never went along with it. She would use the shortened version when quoting others, but she called me by my full name her whole life. So too do some people who have known me since childhood and a few other folks sprinkled her and there for various reasons. I'm quite alright with it.

Anyway, let's get back to the story that we started with.

"Hey Andrew, did you hear the news?" She had just returned home from work, and I was poised for some great bombshell. "Ted Bundy finally quit smoking."

This was a popular joke in early 1989. Ted Bundy had just been executed in Florida. He and my mother were both 42 at the time. They had been born the exact same day, a fact I joked about from time to time over the years.

Such jokes were not uncommon in our relationship. The fact that I remember this one is probably because of the subject and their shared birth date. It was a common occurrence for her to return home from work and share some tasteless joke she'd heard at work that day. This one was relatively tame.

This love of lowbrow humor was a common family trait. My grandmother requested a particular saying on her tombstone featuring her nickname Pud (rhymes with wood, short for "Puddin'"). It read, "Here lies Pud. She was pretty damn good."

I was a pallbearer at her funeral. During the limo ride to the cemetery, my great uncles told dirty jokes. One of them was a song referencing recent news sung to the tune of Dean Martin's "That's Amore":

"When your wife

Takes a knife

And cuts off

Half your life,

That's a Bobbitt."

Anyway, once again let's get back to our story.

"Ted Bundy finally quit smoking." The joke was in reference to his dying in the electric chair, not about tobacco use. I mistakenly interpreted the joke that way for years. (I was 14. Give me a break.)

I thought of that joke a lot when my mother died in 2011. She had tried to quit smoking numerous times since picking up the habit in the late '60s. It took her 20 more years than Ted Bundy, but she had finally quit.

Tell Me, Mama

Content Warning: Death, War, Family Abandonment

I wish I knew more about my mother. She was extremely stoic. She hated having people worry about her. She seemed to have a pathological need to be selfless. She loved everyone so passionately, forgave much too easily, and always tried desperately to convince the world that she was fine.

When she did talk about herself, it was to entertain or encourage. She would tell unflattering stories about herself for laughs. For example, after her first childbirth experience, she received an enema after taking too long to poop. Wanting to avoid that the second time around, she ate a large number of prunes. She ended up shitting all over her hospital room floor and cleaning it up herself out of embarrassment.

But anyway, let's get into some things about her that she told me.

She was born November 24, 1946 (like I mentioned in the previous piece, the exact same day as Ted Bundy). She was the second-oldest of four children my maternal grandparents had together, two boys and two girls. My grandmother's second marriage would produce another baby brother and bring in some step-siblings. Being the oldest daughter in that particular time and place probably instilled in her the maternal habits and instincts she displayed until the end of her life.

Her father left the family when she was still pretty young, though I don't recall exactly how old she was. He spent most of his life after leaving my grandmother in the southern U.S. where he re-married and adopted a child just a few years older than me. I don't know what he did when he lived with my grandmother, but later in life he was a Baptist minister coincidentally sharing a name with a very famous Southern Baptist minister. Most of the family would not see him again until my mother organized a reunion in the mid-1980's.

JFK was shot two days before my mother's 17th birthday during her senior year in high school. She heard the news from a classmate who had heard the news during lunch. I heard this story after the Challenger disaster. I heard about that from my 6th grade teacher who had heard the news during lunch. But I digress.

My mother got married right after high school. Her uncle gave her away since her father wasn't present. Her husband was in the Army and gave her the last name that I carry. She didn't bother changing it after they divorced. (Now I see where I get my laziness from.)

During that marriage, a fun little story occurred that she told me years later: My mother was working for her uncle who was a Justice of the Peace. One day a young man came in to deal with a ticket he received for having a mutilated driver's license. She took his guilty plea and asked why his driver's license was in such a condition. "Ma'am, I just got back from Vietnam," he answered.

After talking some more, she discovered that he had been the door gunner on the helicopter flown by her older brother. Small world.

Toward the end of the marriage, she became pregnant, which might've helped end the marriage. I don't know when the divorce was finalized, but the marriage was definitely over by the time my sister was born in the spring of 1970.

A few years after my sister was born, my mother went to work as a court recorder. It was then she got involved with a judge who would become my father. They never married, but their relationship was over by the time I was born. It was a little like history repeating.

My Father

My mother was careful not to speak ill of my father. I was usually afraid to ask anything. So what I do know mostly comes from snippets of memories from long-ago conversations.

He served in World War II, even before my mother was born. He had been married before and had other kids, six before me.

At least I think it was six. I met most of them at his visitation after he died. All but one knew who I was. We didn't discuss that, but it was clear in the way they looked at me and spoke with me. Only the youngest of my older brothers was unaware of our relationship. They were all nice people. I haven't talked to any of them since. (I suck like that, anxiety and laziness and stuff.)

For a long time I was bitter about my father's abandonment. Though he never failed to pay his child support, we never had a relationship. I heard he saw me several times as a baby, but I would've been unable to recognize him on the street at any point in my life. People who knew him often told me I looked a lot like him.

I understand that lack of a relationship now. As of this writing, I've barely spoken to anyone in my family since my mother's passing. In some cases, it's because we are terrible at staying in touch. In some cases, it's very much a deliberate choice that I have no intention of changing (which I will mostly cover later). In some cases, it's just intense anxiety getting in my way. So it turns out my father may have given me more than his face.

(In the early part of 2019, I got a message through a popular DNA site from my sister from the same mister. We have talked some as I write this in spring 2019. She seems really nice, and I hope I can get past my anxiety to talk to her more.)

I Was Born

When my mother went to bed on St. Patrick's Day 1974, she was well past her due date. She woke up in the wee small hours of the morning feeling nothing below her waist and unable to move her legs. It may have been that I was somehow pressing on her spine. She called her friend Ethel who came over to her apartment in a panic and helped her get to the hospital.

She was still unable to move her legs when they reached the hospital and needed to get her down the stairs to the maternity ward. Unfortunately, the elevators were out of service. So she had to be carried down a flight of stairs in a cafeteria chair. Thought this was probably an unpleasant experience in the moment, she would often laugh about it over the years.

As they finally got her on a table and removed her pants, a nurse cried,

"His head is out!" I was well on my way.

I emerged just fine just before 6 a.m. No father was initially listed on my birth certificate. That was added a few weeks later.

Having an amendment to my birth certificate definitely caused some awkward looks from adults during my school years. It's quite common now, but in the time and place I grew up, single parenting was unusual. In the small town where I moved just before my tenth birthday, I knew nobody in my peer group with a single parent and only one or two who had a step-parent.

There is certainly no one to blame, but that last part was probably another contributor to my long-term mental health issues. I already felt like a freak because of the abuse I had suffered. Having such an obvious difference from all of my peers further contributed to my feelings of isolation.

I'll get to all that later, though. For now, let's finish up with some things my mother told me.

She Worked Hard For the Money

My earliest memory of my mother's working life was as manager of the apartment complex where we lived. Such jobs are never stable. She was fired in a house-cleaning quite typical of the industry when I was 7. Many years later as an adult, I worked a janitorial job with a man who lost his apartment maintenance job in similar fashion. That job was at the exact same complex my mother once managed, still owned by the exact same company.

After a brief period of unemployment, my mother went back to more familiar work as a legal secretary for a local lawyer. When one of the partners in the firm was appointed to a prosecutor's job in the later '80s, the firm dissolved. Her boss joined up with some other lawyers, and they moved into an office upstairs from a credit union. During that time, she started working with other lawyers and eventually became the office manager.

While working that janitorial job I mentioned earlier, I cleaned her office from time to time. A few years and a few jobs later, I became a teller at that credit union, working in that very branch. Even I can't handle all this synchronicity (though it sometimes sucks as you'll read later).

About a decade after that move, one of the lawyers in the firm was appointed to a judicial vacancy. Needing a secretary and court recorder, his choice was easy. My mother was on the move again.

She loved her job at the court but was looking forward to retiring right after she turned 65. Her boss did not want her to retire until he did, but her mind was made up. He's still on the bench as I write this, and she never did retire. She died less than eight months from her milestone birthday.

Things I Could Never Tell My Mother

Part the First:

Childhood Matters

Sissy

I called my sister "Sissy" when I was very young. I adored her, and I loved making her happy. Doing nice things for her used to fill me with such euphoria my voice would quiver. She was the second-most important person in my life behind my mother.

Neither of us ever knew our fathers. That was actually one of the few things we really had in common. We didn't really look alike, and our personalities were quite different. I was quiet, well-behaved, and eager to please. She was loud, showy, and often getting into trouble.

When people who knew her would hear my last name, they would ask if I was her brother. They rarely believed it. "Nuh-uh!" was the most common refrain when I begrudgingly acknowledged our relationship.

In high school, an older girl in my Algebra class told her best friend who my sister was. A rather heated argument ensued between them over whether or not this was a hoax or some kind of joke. I still have no idea what benefit there would've been to lying about such a thing. But I do understand it was hard to believe that she and I were siblings, much less related. Even I didn't always believe it.

Like I said before, I was a good child, and she was often in trouble. She was probably jealous of the positive attention I received, and that helped make me a target for her internal hurt and anger. She often tried to tell me I was stupid, fat, ugly, and anything else that might damage my self-esteem. She was quite successful.

What Happened Before

(When I first wrote these next couple pieces, I had planned on doing a big reveal that I was talking about my sister afterward. There was also a certain element of denial to it, which is common for trauma survivors. We would rather question our own memories than to acknowledge that someone we love has hurt us so deeply. Anyway, please pardon the forthcoming vagueness. I chose not to rewrite these pieces about my sister as that vagueness might be worth reading, particularly considering the underlying reasons.)

When I was a young child, we had a friendly neighborhood handyman. I can't remember his name, but he was quite popular with the neighborhood kids. I'm pretty sure he raped at least one child in our neighborhood, probably multiple. And there's no way to know just how many.

By the time I moved away from that neighborhood just before my 10th birthday, he was long gone. I don't remember when or why he left. At that age, people you don't see every day can easily disappear without you noticing, especially adults. He might've been discovered as a pedophile and gone to jail. He might've just moved away, which I think is much more likely. Again, I don't remember his name so I have no idea what happened to him exactly.

I say I'm pretty sure he raped at least one child because I really don't know. He never touched me inappropriately. My only evidence is the word of an older girl I knew back then. She said she lost her virginity at the age of 10 with this man whose name I can't remember.

It would be easy to doubt her story because she is certainly not a credible witness. Her reputation of telling wild lies and other tall tales was quite widespread and well-earned.

There was something about the way she said it, though, that makes this one story seem believable. She was completely unemotional and directly answering a question posed to her by a peer. While this was just the sort of thing that might inspire one of her tall tales, this one had certain elements that make me believe it.

She was four years older than me which makes the timing of the event four years before I moved away. Again, I have no idea when this left the neighborhood, but he was almost certainly around at the right time and may have even left soon after "taking her virginity".

Another factor lending weight to her accusation is that many people who grew up in that neighborhood remember her as being highly sexual. There could have been other reasons for her learning about sex at such a young age, but this makes me feel even more strongly that she was telling the truth.

Oh, and there's one last thing that makes me believe her, maybe the strongest evidence of all. It's what she did to me.

One Not-So-Fine Day

I think I was 6 years old, but I don't know that for sure. Details like this are hard for trauma survivors to remember, particularly when it happens at such young ages.

I do remember quite clearly where it happened. I remember the room and the bed and all the events of that day as clearly as I remember what I did yesterday, maybe even more clearly.

I was a good boy. Everybody said so. In fact, she was the only one not to praise me regularly. I craved it from her. I would do anything to have her approve of me and love me. So when she wanted to do things that felt really icky, I went along with it.

We took off all our clothes and got on the bed. We touched each other's genitals. She had me get on all fours as she rubbed her genitals on my butt. "That feels really good," she told me. I told her I was glad. My voice was trembling. I was clearly sad and disgusted by what I was doing. She moaned with delight.

Eventually, she had me turn over. I asked her what she wanted, and she just told me that it would feel really good. Luckily, my young age and my fear prevented my body from producing an erection. She gave up quickly and never again asked me for sexual favors. Older boys were readily available, willing, and more suitable to her tastes.

I don't recall her ever telling me not to tell. She didn't need to do that anyway. I knew all of it was wrong. I didn't want her to get in trouble and worried about that for myself as well. After all, I was a good boy. Everybody said so.

A version of this originally appeared on Across the Margin as "When 'It' Happened".

That Girl

Content Warning: Violence, Child Sexual Abuse, Psychological Abuse, Physical Abuse

As much as my sister's abuse scarred me, I think witnessing her abusing others may have taken an even greater toll.

One day she took me along on a baby-sitting job. She was watching the very young daughter of a single mother. I don't know how old this little girl was at the time, but I know she was still in diapers and not yet talking. She might not have even been walking yet. I was probably about 8 years old and my sister 12.

Her abuse of this little girl took two main forms. The first was a role-playing game with us just playing ourselves while she put on a Jekyll-and-Hyde act. She would walk out of the room, put her hair up in a side tail, and return assuming a different identity that was verbally and physically abusive. She called herself by a different in those moments. She would push both of us and hit us until the little girl would cry. She would then walk back out of the room, let down her hair, and resume her "good" persona.

After returning to the room in this "good" persona, she would ask us what happened and comfort us. It gave an illusion of caring to a psychologically abusive situation, and the abuse didn't end there. These comforting moments often led to simulating breastfeeding with this little girl. Even in the moment, I think I was more disgusted by that than by my own sexual abuse.

Many years later in a public speech, I apologized to that little girl for not saying something and maybe stopping the abuse. I've never forgotten her first name, but I never knew her last name and have no idea where she is now. She's probably in her 30's as I write this. Anytime I meet a woman of a similar age with the same name, I stop and wonder if it might be her.

I can only hope she was too young to remember any of the awful things

that were done to her. I won't reveal
her name, but I do want to apologize
to her again. I'm sorry. I know I was
too young to be responsible, but I
still wish I had said something. I
hope your life turned out
wonderfully.

Helpless

My mother spent a number of years living with a man she met sometime in the early '80s. In the early years of their relationship, he had quite a drinking problem. Ultimately, he got help and stayed sober for the rest of their time together. Unfortunately, as is usually the case, bad things happened to inspire that change.

He came home late. He was drunk. I think it was his birthday. My mother was unhappy because she had plans that he had blown off so that he could drink at a bar. This was not the first time this sort of thing had happened.

That was one of my mother's great faults, one she passed onto me. She often loved to the point of enabling.

I was already awake when they started yelling at each other. I don't know how many times he hit her. I think it was twice. Maybe it was three times. The next day she had two black eyes and was missing at least two front teeth. For months, she would self-consciously cover her mouth while talking. She didn't want anyone seeing the gap at the bottom of her mouth.

I never told my mother that I heard everything. I pretended that I slept through the whole ordeal. I wished I had. I certainly hated lying in bed feeling helpless, but I was just a prepubescent kid. I had no idea what to do, except add one more thing to my guilt list of things to carry for years on end. They tend to have a common theme: helplessness. And the one time in childhood I chose not to be helpless had more damaging effects.

I Didn't Know What a Brute I Was

My sister rarely hit me. That might leave marks and let everyone find out the truth about her. People thought she was a great baby-sitter. All the kids in her charge were always so well-behaved. Some of that is because we were all just good kids. Some of that is because we were scared to death of her.

We tend to have a limited view of violence, but it's not limited to actions that actually cause injury. As I said, she rarely hit me, though she wasn't shy about physically restricting movement and pinning down smaller kids, including and especially me. Her favorite form of violence was making threats, and she often supplemented her words with weapons.

My childhood best friend to this day ascribes his pyrophobia to her repeatedly flicking a lighter or matches in his face. For me, her preferred weapon was a knife. She would often brandish one if I was non-compliant.

Once when I was around 10 or 11, she was unable to find her new blouse and somehow thought I might've taken it. She pinned me to the couch, knife in her hand right next to my face, and screamed, "I'm going to kill you, mother fucker! I will fucking kill you!" I cried and begged for my life, swearing I didn't take it.

That was the truth. I didn't take it. Before having my life threatened, I didn't even know she had a new blouse.

My sister was often living elsewhere as puberty brought the growth spurts that would make me bigger than her. During her stretches living at home then, her use of knives increased as she no longer had a size advantage. One summer day when I was 14, we had what was admittedly a petty argument over what to watch on TV. The subject was irrelevant, though. I had reached my breaking point.

It wasn't really about the TV channel. It was about not giving up my power any longer. I refused to be intimidated any longer. I refused to let her rule my life. When she went to the kitchen to grab her favorite knife, I ran into my bedroom and grabbed my baseball bat.

It scares me to know how prepared I was to use it. I even hit her hand when she tried to grab the bat. I was prepared to fight to the death.

She backed away and called the police who made me put the bat back in my room. She never threatened me with a knife again.

Years later I realized she was too cowardly to follow through with her threats. I was the only one prepared to actually fight.

I spent years haunted with knowing how close I was to killing my sister. It made me afraid to be angry. I bottled up that emotion and even more for decades.

A version of this originally appeared on The Honeyed Quill as "The Beast Within Me".

Part the Second:

Motherless Child

Sundays Will Never Be the Same

On a lazy Sunday afternoon in Afghanistan in April of 2011, I stood by helplessly and watched a man bleeding to death (a story told later). The following Sunday morning I was informed my mother had died.

She spent her last three months between a hospital and rehab center dealing with a variety of ailments. These included congestive heart failure that she kept secret from everyone she could, including me. It was just like when she covered her mouth to hid her missing teeth. She didn't like people worrying about her. So none of us were prepared for the heart attack that took her life.

During her time in various medical facilities, she repeatedly expressed her wish to go home. Due to fluid build-up in her legs, she was unable to walk and required assistance to live at home. I could've provided some of that assistance. Instead I was on the other side of the world, standing by helplessly and watching a man bleed to death.

I Dream a Dream of Home

It took me two days just to get out of Khost Province. Rain makes the old Soviet airstrips too slick for airplanes to land. There were no helicopter flights or convoys heading to Bagram or any intermediate stop. So April showers kept me grounded.

I spent one of those days not only stuck but also cut off from home. We were on blackout until another Stateside family was notified that their loved one would be coming home early, hailed as a hero.

"Hero" is how we often referred to the fallen. When someone uses the word for me, I become instantly uncomfortable, sometimes even angry. I got to come home alive. Keep that word away from me.

It was Thursday afternoon when I finally made it home, more than 100 hours after I had been notified.

I immediately but nervously headed to my mother's house. Her boyfriend and I had a strained relationship for years, but the present circumstances helped us set our differences aside. Within a couple of hours of touching down in my hometown, still wearing the gaudy clothes I borrowed in Kuwait, I was at the funeral home, making arrangements.

Since I hadn't yet taken my mid-tour leave, I got 25 days to spend at home to bury my mother and take care of estate business. Anyone who's had to deal with an estate can tell you that's not nearly enough time to accomplish much. Add into that I was not my mother's only child. I was just the only responsible one. Even if they would've been helpful, my sister was living in another state, and my nephew was in jail. I was severely limited in what I could do, but the burden clearly fell on my shoulders.

Further complicating matters was the lack of a will. My mother had spent many years working in probate and estate law. I know she had a will. She told me so. Her boss told me he helped her draft one. It was not on file in the county she lived in or the one she worked in. I did hear that someone who was to receive nothing found her will in her home filing cabinet. It would not surprise me if it had been destroyed.

It quickly became clear to me that I couldn't possibly even get a proper start on settling her estate in the time I had. Though she was by no means wealthy, she had dealt in antiques for a number of years which meant she had a lot of stuff. There was no way I could deal with all that in the time allotted.

So I left things for when I would return home sometime around the New Year. A little while after I returned to Afghanistan, my sister showed up in town and tried to take over administration of the estate. I offered to support an alternate administrator, but no one was willing.

I get it. It's a terrible job, and I wouldn't want to take it on for anyone else, much less for a contentious family like mine. I couldn't fight a court battle from a combat zone 7000 miles away, and so I gave up the fight.

Although she managed to steal a number of items from my mother's home, my sister failed in her estate takeover attempt. With protests from my nephew and others, the judge refused her request and appointed an independent lawyer to handle my mother's estate.

My sister, nephew, and I all submitted survivor claims. I put in an additional $8000 claim for funeral and burial costs which superseded all the inheritance rights. It was the one card I held to try and fulfill my mother's wishes.

The law required that the lawyer administering the estate get paid first. Everyone else got whatever they could steal, and I received a $250 check for those funeral and burial costs.

Part the Third:

Addiction and Stuff

Turn the Other Way

Despite the many things I've recounted previously, my sister and I did manage to have a civil relationship into the 1990s. We were actually friendly when she became pregnant with her first child and gave birth in December 1989. I was a proud uncle and especially excited to have a nephew.

This may come as a surprise, but my sister was not a good mother. As her marriage was falling apart in the spring of 1990, she came back home. When they arrived, my nephew was showing some distinct signs of neglect. This led to a number of arguments between my sister and mother.

One day when my nephew was just over five months old, it all came to a head. I was on summer break from school. My sister came banging on my bedroom door and telling me, "Come take care of your little brother." She had decided to give up custody and was leaving. I would spend most of the summer baby-sitting him.

We were quite close for much of the next several years. We had tons of fun together. He invited me to school with him for his last day of fifth grade. I was his hero. I loved the living shit out of it and him.

Of course, I was not the greatest uncle ever. I was extremely depressed and wasn't always as available as I wished I was. (That's difficult when you're sleeping or trying to sleep much of your life away.) By the time he was an adolescent, I was away from home and not coming around too often. We were drifting apart, and he was drifting toward drugs.

He did the things that addicts tend to do: lie, cheat, steal, whatever it took to get high. He would be in and out of jail. Occasionally, he would get clean and make people think maybe he was fulfilling his promise. Anyone who has ever dealt with an addict can relate to this story. It happens all the time, and always cycles right back to the things that addicts do.

Some of the things he did while high including assaulting my mother (while I was in basic training luckily for him) and stealing from me the day I left for Iraq. My mom's boyfriend was pissed at me when I turned him in. That tune changed after about the tenth time it happened to him.

I gave him one last chance after my mother died. Of course, he fucked that right up. I have been tempted from time to time to talk to him. But everything I hear from him shows all the signs that he is still very much in his addiction, whether he's using substances or not. It sucks, but I've learned the hard way. Including from myself.

Falling In Love
with Booze

Content Warning: Substance Abuse, Alcoholism

When I was very young, I would sometimes steal sips from my mother's beverages at family gatherings. Sometimes the taste was strange, and I'd ask her what it was. "Booze," she'd reply. It wasn't my favorite, but I didn't mind it so much.

As time went on, she drank alcohol less and less. She explained to me that my father was an alcoholic. She quit completely around the time she reconciled with her now-sober boyfriend. Also around that time I pretty well decided that I would never drink.

That was pretty easy all throughout high school. Plenty of people drank, but all the attention paid to peer pressure seemed effective. Everyone was quite polite and understanding on the few occasions I was offered and refused alcohol. When I started college, though, that peer pressure education started fading away.

It wasn't that anyone really pushed alcohol, but I was offered it a lot more often. Some of my friends who rarely or never drank in high school started drinking like normal college students. (I haven't known any of them to develop a drinking problem fortunately.) I still resisted, though, at least for a while.

I drank some on my 21st birthday, but it still didn't appeal to me. I drank very small amounts here and there after that but still had never been drunk. I tried from time to time, but I couldn't find a drink that really appealed to me. Then in the summer of my 22nd year, I finally discovered something I liked: hard cider.

I forget the brand, but it doesn't really matter anyway. This stuff didn't really feel like drinking alcohol. It was sweet and pleasant. I drank away absent-mindedly, not feeling any real effects. But when I got up to go to the bathroom, I realized I had a buzz. And I liked it.

Soon after I found a particular brand that I especially enjoyed. I would usually buy myself a six-pack early in the week and look forward to drinking it down over the weekend. We had quite the loving affair for a few years, but over time I started to get acquainted with another would-be lover: vodka.

I made sure to be careful (such a typical addict lie) as I was developing this love. I only drank about once a week, typically on a designated bar night. Also to prove my control, I would give up drinking completely for certain periods of time. I would go on the wagon a couple months here and there, giving myself until a particular date or a certain number of days. I did 100 days at one point.

Soon after completing these sober stretches, I would jump, not fall, off the wagon. Forcefully. I didn't just get a buzz. I was getting obnoxiously drunk. But that sober stretch beforehand would convince me that I was in control.

I think the last hard cider I drank was after one of these stretches on the wagon. Watching a friend destroy his life with alcohol had scared me into one of my abstinence periods. I did over 200 days that time. Then one night some co-workers were having a party, and I decided to stop by with a quart of my favorite hard cider. I figured I could keep it cool, hang out a while, and be able to drive home. Silly me.

Someone asked if I wanted to do a shot, and I figured a shot of vodka would be safe. But the first shot was tequila. Dissatisfied, I requested a shot of vodka. The next one was gin. I wasn't about to stop until I got the vodka I wanted. And then when I did get it, I had a couple more.

At that point, I was good and drunk. I got so drunk, in fact, that at one point I just fell down. I didn't trip over anything. No external force disturbed my balance. I just fell on my ass like an uncoordinated toddler. You'd think that would wake me up, but no.

I kept selling myself some of the classic alcoholic lies. I didn't drink alone. I tried that once. It didn't really do anything for me. Drinking helped me overcome social anxiety, and with no one around, there just didn't seem to be a point.

I didn't drink every day. I limited it to designated bar nights and occasional weekend parties. If circumstances cancelled a bar night, I would feel antsy the whole the next week. At the time, though, I didn't recognize this as a sign of addiction.

The amount I was drinking somehow didn't bother me either. I was taking down a fifth of vodka at parties. I had no idea how much I was drinking at the club. None of this mattered to me anyway. I figured it took like 20 years to become an alcoholic, and that time wouldn't come until my 40s.

The realization of how wrong I was came when I was 28. History repeated, and I went to a party put on by some co-workers, intending only to have a couple of drinks. One of my young co-workers had never had vodka, and I thought I'd do her a favor and share some with her.

(In case you're getting any ideas, this was not a predatory thing. I had no romantic interest in her. I had my eyes on another at the time. I really was just trying to be nice.)

The sharing didn't happen. Once I got started, I didn't stop. I drank the whole bottle myself in under two hours.

My body was pissed. I puked violently in the backyard. I collapsed next to my pile. I thought I was going to die.

Some nice boys picked me up and tossed me on a spare bed in the basement. When I woke up, I came to grips with the fact that I had a problem. I decided I was going to quit drinking.

The day had all kinds of synchronistic qualities to it. It was June 15, 2002, Harry Nilsson's 61st birthday. He was an old favorite of mine. I heard him on the radio the night he died, a block of "Without You", "Coconut", and "I Guess the Lord Must Be in New York City". He had a heart attack in January 1994 caused largely by many years of drinking.

It seemed fitting this would be the day I quit drinking. It probably helped me hold onto sobriety longer than I would have without it.

Jumping Back Into the Fire Water

It was about five years before my next drink, but it is true that once you start again, it's as if you never stopped.

It happened in the summer of 2007. I was at the U.S. Army Intelligence School at Ft. Huachuca, Arizona, a long, long ways from home, and life wasn't going as planned. My security clearance was on hold because when I was young, dumb, and depressed, I wasn't very good at paying my bills. My friends were scattering away to their duty stations and getting orders for deployments. I had joined to serve, not languish at a training post. I decided to give up the fight, at least the one against alcohol.

Since I didn't have a car, there was no need to worry about drunk driving. I got shit-faced with people several times and had a bunch of fun. I even got a nice story out of it as a chaplain I knew picked me up when he saw me walking down the road on a Sunday morning, hungover and unable to find a cab.

It was a few weeks of drunken fun that I could keep secret from all the people who knew me to be sober. When the time came for me to move on to my next stop, I quit drinking once again. I figured this would be like a little fling never to be repeated. That lasted about two years.

After surviving Iraq, I decided it was time for some fun once again. I already had orders for my next stop, so I figured this would be just another temporary thing. I frequented a bar in Colorado Springs and enjoyed many drunken good times. When I left Ft. Carson toward the end of 2009, I got back on the wagon once again.

I remained that way for the next couple years as I relocated to Ft. Knox and prepared for my second deployment.

I spent almost all of 2011 in Afghanistan. It was a rough year, and when the time was coming to head home, I knew it would be much like coming home from Iraq.

I got blissfully drunk that first night home. I had a scary moment after I locked myself out of a friend's room where I had left my booze. I made an excuse about his oven being on to convince the duty sergeant to let me back in. I wasn't lying. He had a pot roast in the oven. He was pissed at me for turning it off, but I got my vodka and drank it all up.

I drank several more times over the next couple of months. My last time wasn't planned to be my last time. I went to a birthday celebration and had a couple of drinks at a restaurant. Later we went bowling and smuggled in some liquor. I was prepared to share my vodka, but I drank almost all of it, just like the night that first inspired me to quit drinking.

Soon after that night, several of my friends left on orders for other places. Without those drinking buddies around, I quit again.

That would've been in March of 2012. I haven't had a drink since. Part of that is being back around a lot of people who are aware of my problem. Part of that is being anti-social and not being invited to events where I'm likely to drink. None of that is lack of temptation. I have been tempted many times, but I've been lucky to stay dry.

(I believe I wrote that in the summer of 2015. I jumped off the wagon again some months later. I quit once more when the springtime came again and have stayed that way as of this writing. I make no promises about it being permanent, though. I've finally learned to do it one day at a time.)

I've Got Calling Cards

Content Warning: Drugs, Addiction, Suicide, Death

I began this section discussing enabling, and I'm going to end it that way too. After all, that habit of mine is probably much worse than my addictions. At the very least, it eats at me a whole lot more.

I've written previously about a good friend I had in the Army, and you'll read about him more later. He spoke often of having been addicted to drugs and losing many friends to drugs. This was part of what blinded me to the warning signs when he stayed at my house, helping me to sell it in the spring of 2016.

I mean, I noticed the large amount of beer he was drinking. And I was aware that he was on a lot of prescriptions, particularly for pain.

These things alone should've been enough, but when you're close to someone, you often want to ignore the signs. I definitely did with my nephew.

There were other little things I had seen over the previous few years too. There were emotional breakdowns, the weird bouts of anxiety over silly things, the strange requests to borrow money, so many little things. Much of this I attributed solely to PTSD, but looking back, I should've realized there was more.

His family has never revealed how he died. That's typical when a servicemember or veteran commits suicide, but you learn to read between the lines. And between those lines, I could see that he had killed himself with a drug overdose, perhaps intentional, perhaps not. It doesn't really matter. The end result is the same: my friend is dead, and I helped make it happen.

I know it's not my fault, but it hurts all the same. I loaned him money. I let him stay in my house. I saw all the signs, and I didn't intervene. Chances are he would've killed himself regardless of what I did. Still, I will carry this lesson with me forever.

Part the Fourth:

Who's Afraid of Virginia Woolf?

Sex, Lies, And Sexuality

Content Warning: Non-Explicit Sex

When I started having those teenage feelings, I was physically attracted to girls just like your typical heterosexual adolescent boy. The problem was my sexual abuse made me horribly uncomfortable with any though of physical intimacy. Even the word "vagina" gave me the shivers. I couldn't stand to look at them. The idea of touching one filled me with dread and disgust. As my peers became more and more sexually active, I was staying in my shell.

There were a couple of girls I really liked who may have liked me. There was a girl I had a class with in 8th grade whom I thought was really pretty, but I was always too afraid to talk to her. During my freshman year of high school, I had a class with a sophomore girl who came by smiling one day. I was so terrified that I gave a polite wave and went back to work. This was a regular pattern for me for many years. A lot of girls really liked me, but I knew eventually we'd have to do those "icky" things.

I did finally allow myself to date a few girls through my 20's. I kissed a couple of them, but things never went too far. Touching a breast was like going to the moon. No one had to worry about me taking it much further. At least one girl even broke up with me because she thought this meant I was uninterested.

Letting someone touch me was even more out of the question. Not many even tried. I would typically sabotage a relationship long before we got there. I was a 20-something-year-old virgin, but this story was not one that would make for a hit movie.

The older I got, the more ashamed I felt over my inability to have sex. I knew there was nothing wrong with me physically. It was purely emotional, and I thought that was inexcusable. My biggest shame isn't even that I remained a virgin for so long. It's the lies and half-truths I told to cover it up.

In my late 20's, I was briefly involved with a woman named Sara Dexter. She was an old friend of mine, but we kept things somewhat casual. We were at uncertain points in our lives, and she was considering leaving town. Eventually, she went off to school in Chicago, and we drifted apart. We had a nice, non-serious relationship that one could assume included regular sex.

The only problem was Sara Dexter didn't exist. She was little more than a shield to avoid questions and keep away anyone who might be interested. Only a couple of people in the world had any clue I even might be a virgin, and I just wanted people to think I was normal.

Which Will

I met her on a Monday in the summer of 2000. Actually, I don't know the exact day of the week, but it sounded good and helped me figure out how to start this topic off.

She was involved with someone else when we first met. So I didn't really consider her a girlfriend possibility. We became close friends, and I cared for her very deeply. I just didn't think our relationship would take the route that it did.

She admitted years later that she knew she was in love with me soon after we first met. I'm sure I loved her long before I knew, but I knew her for almost two years before admitting it to myself. Even when I did, I didn't think I had a shot at competing with the other guy. So I stayed silent until it seemed that relationship was coming to an end.

One night we had a long talk about relationships. We shared a very long hug, and she gave me a long, deep kiss on the cheek. Pulling back slightly, she whispered, "I almost kissed you."

"It's okay," I replied. "You can if you want to." We looked at each other for a while. My anxiety began to rise, and I began to pull away. She put her hand on my cheek and softly whispered my name. Pulling me back toward her, we kissed for the first time.

It was soft but passionate. I didn't have a lot of experience at kissing, but I just let my instincts take over. I loved her, and I tried my best to express that.

"Wow," she said as she pushed me away slightly. We shared more kisses and cuddled a while. My heart pounding wildly, I asked her what she wanted me to do after this night together. "Just be there," she said. I won't claim to have always been successful at that, but I always tried.

As we prepared to depart, I wrapped her up for one last long, passionate kiss. It was one she would cite often in our ensuing relationship. It was easily my most aggressive move of the evening. I realized later that I could've easily groped her multiple times, but my hands never reached for anything but her face, her shoulders, and her back. I don't think it occurred to me then to try. I was probably afraid to try anything else, but it made me proud to have had such a purely romantic evening with her.

Roller Coaster of Love

Content Warning: Semi-Explicit Sex

Sometime in the middle of my Army career, my old roommate described my relationship with my then-girlfriend thusly, "You had a thing, and then you didn't have a thing, and then you kind of had a thing, and then you really didn't have a thing, and now it seems you have a thing." It was a beautiful run-on sentence that perfectly described the ups and downs of our relationship.

After the night of that first kiss, we had a very passionate fling for a few months. During that time, I told her about my abuse history and my complete lack of consensual history. While she was careful to not push me for sex, she did express a strong desire to be my first.

It was perhaps the third time we kissed that she finally guided my hand to her breasts. She was amazed at the gentleness of my touch, saying it was as if I was afraid to touch her. She was correct in that assumption. About two and a half months after our first kiss, I found the courage to please her. I was not then ready to let her touch me in a similar way or even take off my clothes for her.

She told me later that encounter gave her new confidence in herself. She confronted the guy she had been seeing when we met. He owned up to all his faults and told her he still loved her. That led them to rekindle their old romance.

I received the news in a cryptic email. We had another conversation over the phone and a much more painful one in person where she made it clear that she was in love with him. We remained friends for a while and then drifted apart. Months later we had a brief spat and cut off contact. That was the end of our first attempt.

I hadn't talked to her in over a year when a crisis inspired me to seek her out. We met for coffee one night and started making another go at being friends. She told me she dropped that other guy, but in my emotional state, I wasn't thinking that we might take another chance at our own romance.

Over dinner a couple weeks later I noticed her avoidance of eye contact. She fidgeted with a napkin wrapper, and I grabbed her hand. Our eyes met, and we realized we still had feelings for each other. As she dropped me off back at my house, I tried to kiss her. She pulled away. I apologized and got out of her car.

Our next conversation was uncomfortable, and we both avoided sustained eye contact. It became clear to me this wasn't going to work. She was an addiction for me, just like alcohol. It was also clear to me that she had issues she needed to deal with. As I cut off contact with her again, I encouraged her to seek help. Looking back, that was a boundary I should've maintained, but I've never been that wise.

Late in the summer after I enlisted, I found a new excuse to reach out to her. I'd been unsuccessful in another romantic pursuit and decided to reach out to some old flames to understand how I kept sabotaging relationships. (I called it my "High Fidelity" project after the Nick Hornby novel that inspired my quest.)

She was the only one to respond. I figured it was safe for us to talk because I was a couple thousand miles away. I was wrong. After a week or so, I came to realize what she already knew: the flame was still very much alive for both of us.

Over the next three months we managed to stay in touch through our typical cycle of highs and lows, belief and doubt. The distance may have been beneficial. Had we been able to get physical any earlier, we likely would've run away from each other once again. Instead we forged a very deep bond by the time I was back home on leave.

The First Time

There was no doubt we were going to have sex for the first time when I came home. It had been almost five-and-a-half years since our first kiss, but we were still careful not to rush into things. When I finally saw her in person, I squeezed her and cried, "It's really you."

We sat on the couch and kissed passionately. Clothes started coming off as we became re-acquainted physically. When our hands began to reach below each other's waists, we stopped. I suggested we move to the bed. We removed the rest of our clothes along the way. She was eager, but I sat there nervously. "I don't know what to do," I admitted shyly. She smiled at me and helped me gently. When it was over, we cuddled and cried together.

I was 33 years old and thought I had finally become a normal human being. I was wrong about that. I had always been normal, just damaged by trauma. And all that I had invested in this experience made me hang on for much longer than I should have.

Jealous Girl

Content Warning: Rape, Child Sexual Abuse, Emotional Abuse, Physical Abuse

I have a hard time trusting myself. I fell for my ex-girlfriend in part because she seemed to put so much trust in me, but in the end, it was clear that was never the case. She never really trusted me.

I had never dated a woman born after the Carter Administration, but she was constantly worried about younger women. It didn't matter how much I told her she was beautiful. Saying I didn't want to be with anyone else meant nothing.

She was well aware that she was the only woman I'd ever given myself to so completely. I couldn't understand how she'd think I could so easily give myself to someone else, particularly someone young enough (theoretically anyway) to be my child.

This is an especially difficult problem considering I have several friends who are attractive younger women. Wanting to find myself a new sister has certainly pushed me to seek out friendships with women. To turn these relationships sexual would ruin all of that. I tried to explain this and empathize with my ex-girlfriend's fear, but after a while, I just couldn't do it anymore.

Of course, I did find other ways to assuage her insecurity. I isolated myself more and more. My general PTSD-related anxiety helped with that, but some of that was just wanting to avoid the hassle of her jealousy. I had several close friends that I didn't speak to, some of them for years. Many are probably gone for good.

The worst happened a little over a year before we finally fell apart for good. I was working at a youth homeless shelter then. One morning we took in a sweet, scared little 14-year-old girl. She had been neglected and abused emotionally, physically, and sexually. Her story was heartbreaking, but I tried my best to help her feel safe.

When she arrived at the shelter, she was afraid to eat, sleep, or bathe. During my shift her first night there, I told her repeatedly that she was in a safe place staffed by people who would protect and care for her. Within those eight hours, she ate a little, she showered, and she went to bed. She told me afterward that she only slept a couple of hours, but I was so happy for the progress we made.

Because we were so short-handed at the time, I was working every night. This little girl always got extremely agitated at bedtime, and I always did my best to calm her nerves. I would keep reminding her that she was in a safe place.

Through some of our conversations, I came to realize that virtually every man she had ever known had raped her. So on her fifth night at the shelter, when she asked me for a hug, I broke the rules, and I gave her one. Even now, I cry thinking about it.

When I told my ex-girlfriend about this the next day, I could see the jealousy in her face. I was shocked and angry. How could she think this? This girl was a child. My ex-girlfriend knew my history, knew my fear of becoming a monster. How could she think this?

"It's not your boundaries I worry about," she explained. "It's hers."

I've tried desperately to figure out the logic. This little girl weighed perhaps half as much as me. While she was tough and scrappy, she had no chance of overpowering me. She would also have a nearly impossible time drugging me and then having her way with me, especially since there was always at least one other staff member on duty. So that pretty well eliminates the possibility of her raping me. Besides, my ex-girlfriend surely wouldn't consider it cheating if I were raped. So what was making her so jealous?

The only real explanation would be that my ex-girlfriend thought my worst fear was true. The only way I could possibly cheat on my ex-girlfriend with a 14-year-old girl would be to rape that child. Never mind the fact that I would kill myself before even thinking about doing such a thing.

You must also toss out the heartbreak I felt that all the men in her life had treated her as a sex toy. Forget the pride I felt in making her feel safe. All that was a lie. This person who knew me better than anyone

in the world thought I was a monster.
How could I not think it might be true?

That conversation tore my soul to
shreds. A part of me knew it was over
between us that day. I just didn't know
how to end it. I had spent so much time
trying to convince her of my loyalty
and my determination never to give up
on her. She was making me into a liar.
Despite all that, it took me another
year to finally do the right thing.

Sounds and Silence

I didn't plan the end. It just kind of happened. I'm sure my ex-girlfriend saw it coming, but I wasn't even looking. One day in the summer of 2014, the last straw was placed, and I broke.

The thing people often fail to realize about the last straw is it's often not anything large. It's usually some small thing that wouldn't normally cause the camel's back to break. It's all the other shit piled up before that last straw that causes the last breakdown.

There was the jealous, of course. As I wrote earlier, that had led to our relationship being almost completely broken already. But that wasn't everything.

Many straws were placed by her constantly belittling herself. That is a problem by itself, but on top of that, every accomplishment of mine was somehow an indictment of her. When something good would happen in my life, the subject would turn to why I would be with such a loser.

She spoke often of hating the town where we lived and wanting to leave. Sometimes that negativity turned to suicidal talk. No need for me to worry about moving again. She just might kill herself instead.

I tried so hard to be there for her. I wanted her to be happy, but it was clear that I couldn't help her. Making myself happy only made her more miserable. And that in itself made me miserable.

The last straw came one morning while I was out walking with my kitty. I sent her a text joking about my kitty driving me crazy and that maybe I should trade her in for something calmer. She answered with a series of messages that began with anxiety about her own cat, continued with passive aggressive comments about people giving up their cats, and ending with a reminder of how much she hated living in the area and implying suicide.

I thought very briefly about replying, and then realized I had nothing to say. I was done. I ghosted her. It was the only way I knew I could make it happen.

It was a shitty way to end things. I could've done it better. I should've done it better. But it was definitely something that needed to be done.

Part the Fifth:

This Army Life

Enlistment Blues

When I decided I wanted to enlist in the Army (the why comes later), I figured I should get myself into shape. So the day after Thanksgiving 2006, I went to the gym and got on a treadmill. I ran less than 20 minutes and don't know how I survived. I stayed with it, though, and by the time I called a recruiter at the end of the following January, I was confident I could handle the physical demands.

I had a very nice meeting with my recruiter who gave me a practice ASVAB test. I did pretty well on that and scheduled the real thing for the next week. I did even better on the real thing, scoring in the top percentile. All doors were open for me, and I had been thinking I wanted to work in intelligence. The one drawback was that I would have to leave town in two weeks.

The next morning I told my bosses, even before I told my mother. That uncomfortable conversation was coming that night. I couldn't even give two weeks' notice. A week was my limit, and I'd be missing some of that time for enlistment-related events. I would be missing my scheduled Saturday, in fact, to take my physical.

That night I made the trip to give my mother the news. I danced around it for a while. I told her I had a new job that would require me to leave town. She seemed intrigued until I told her, "I've accepted a position as an intelligence analyst with the U.S. Army."

Her face did not betray her panic. "You can't," she said. "You have bad knees." She got up from the table and started to walk outside. I followed her as she lit up a cigarette. I asked how she was feeling. "I'm fine. Just give me a minute to let this sink in." She was lying, but her stoic face took over.

My friends were a mixed bag of freaked out, proud, and confused. Regardless of anyone's feelings, I was on my way. A couple nights before I departed, we gathered at our favorite bar to sing our favorite songs and make fools of ourselves. Well, I bet the songs were mostly favorites of mine. And I was definitely the most prominent fool. But none of this was new.

On February 22, 2007, I swore my oath one more time and boarded a plane for Fort Jackson, South Carolina. I was in the Army then.

Reasons Why

I never thought about enlisting until I realized it didn't matter. Two of my uncles served in Vietnam. Many of their peers burned their draft cards. None of them, the ones who stayed or went, extended or shortened that war by a single day.

I didn't go to war out of belief in a cause or a desire to do violence. I had understood the rationale and supported the war in Afghanistan. I opposed the war in Iraq. Again, though, it didn't matter how I felt about either one. I realized my choice to have my place taken for me or by me, and I didn't want anyone taking my place.

That still leaves the question of how this debate even entered my mind.

In a way, you can blame it on John Mellencamp and Muhammad Ali.

I was riding my exercise bike in my little East Lansing apartment, watching TV (a football game, I think). A commercial came one, I believe for Chevy trucks or something similar. John Mellencamp sang a line about standing and fighting. The line was accompanied first by soldiers firing artillery and then some classic footage of Ali. I started thinking about how Ali had refused to go to Vietnam, and the wheels started turning.

Now don't get me wrong. I bear no ill will to Muhammad Ali. He paid a heavy price for his decision. I understand his refusal to be drafted and can even commend him for using his celebrity to draw attention to the matter. I am no Muhammad Ali.

My decision to stay home or go to war would make no real difference. So when I called the recruiter, I knew I was signing myself up to go to war. I was fully prepared to die. Part of me even hoped for it.

I did two combat tours, one each in Iraq and Afghanistan. Iraq was a long stretch of working harder than I ever thought possible. Our crusty old First

Sergeant told us repeatedly that he was going to take us all over there and bring us all back. He kept his promise. Looking back now, I have immense pride about that. My next deployment would not be so lucky.

Afghanistan started out pretty nicely. There was indirect fire here and there, but pretty soon I had the good fortune of rolling out on a detachment to a quiet little mountaintop base. It was built around an old cemetery, so no boom-booms ever fell out of the sky. It was two glorious months of relative peace. (The gate was hit by a truck bomb some months later, but I was lone gone by that point.) About a week after going back to the big home base, that peace was shattered when I watched some damn office jockey take my place. (The full story will come in a little bit.)

Let's Have a Round for This Soldier

Content Warning: Blood, War, Death

Sometimes when people learn I'm a veteran, they ask how many people I've killed. For a long time, I refused to answer the question. Now I give a number. It's not a random number. It is precise and very meaningful, but it's not the number they're looking for. If they push the matter further, I even give them names.

I spent a couple of years visiting hospice patients, and one of them was a gunner on an aircraft carrier during the Korean War. He shot down dozens, if not hundreds of planes. At least that many men died as a result of his actions. "They were just like me, just guys fighting for their country," he said. "It was them or me and my buddies."

He didn't make the decision to kill anybody. We who fight the wars never do. Those who start the wars make that decision, and they should carry the count of lives lost. We who fight only do our best to make sure the ones who must die are not our brothers and sisters fighting along with us. The number I carry is for those brothers and sisters I've lost. (That number will come later.)

Only one from that number was actually a combat death. A rocket dropped on the road behind him as he was walking back from lunch. Normally, we hear a horrid sound first, but that day we only heard the boom.

There was no alarm at first. We just ran to a bunker after the explosion, dirt and gravel raining down on us. We sat there for a couple minutes and still heard no alarm. Loud noises were an everyday occurrence. It could've been many different things. So we left the bunker, thinking all was well. I had noticed some people running down the road, though, and I wandered in that direction.

As I got closer, I realized there were at least two people down. I heard someone trailing behind me asking about first aid supplies. "Yes!" I yelled back. "Grab the CLS[1] bag!"

As I drew closer, I saw a man I couldn't recognize lying on the ground with a small pool of blood and a spot on his back. Then I noticed a couple of people helping someone up. It was our training room NCO[2].

She was clearly disoriented with blood in her hair and streaming down her arm and leg. I turned to my young partner and told him to run the news to the company about our injured comrade. Just after he departed, I heard the name of the man on the ground. It was our XO[3].

Knowing there was nothing else I could do at that point, I took off to deliver the second half of the news. As I reached the company headquarters, the incoming alarm finally began to sound. It had been several minutes, and the injured people were already in a truck on their way to the hospital.

The office was empty, and as the alarm continued sounding, we took cover in a bunker with some other soldiers from our company. I delivered the news about who was injured, but added, "I'm pretty sure they'll both survive." While there was quite a bit of blood, it didn't seem heavy enough to be fatal. I was correct in one case.

After the all clear sounded, we stumbled around in shock for a couple minutes. Soon a call came in from the hospital for blood donations. Everyone with even a compatible type quickly piled into a truck to rush off to the hospital. By the time we got there, they were already starting to turn people away. Only exact matches were even being considered. Eventually, they sent us all home.

One of our buddies was clearly shaken and being tended to by his best friend. His and the XO's wives were best friends. We did our best to keep ourselves distracted, but soon the word came for us to gather back at the hospital again.

As we walked down the road, we saw a couple women from our company talking to an NCO from the battalion office. We couldn't hear what was said, but the two women immediately began to sob and hug each other. We didn't ask them what they heard. We didn't want to know even though it was obvious.

It took several more minutes for everyone to reach the hospital and hear the inevitable news from our commander. LT did not make it. He had suffered massive internal bleeding that could not be stopped quickly enough.

We sat around a while, consoling our most upset friends and trying to fix up our own brave faces. We had all participated in airfield ceremonies before, giving final salutes to the fallen as they're loaded onto an aircraft for their trip home. This one would be far more difficult.

I lined up across from a mountain of a man who was also one of the kindest human beings I knew. We made eye contact very briefly but had to break it to prevent losing our bearing. Next to him was a medic who had worked on our comrades, blood still on his leg and sock. He had been wearing PTs[4] at work. It was Sunday after all. Light duty day.

[1]*Combat Life Saver*

[2]*NCO = Non-Commissioned Officer, i.e. corporals and sergeants. The training room NCO has a thankless job keeping records and doing a lot*

of annoying work for company officers and senior NCOs.

[3]Executive Officer, second in command

[4]Physical Training. PTs refers to the physical fitness uniform, T-shirt and shorts in warm weather.

Let's Have a Round for These Friends of Mine

Content Warning: Blood, War, Death

The first comrade I carry on my number was one I never went to war with. We had each gone separately, but he died a few months before we were to go together. He was our training room NCO. He was a beefy man just shy of six feet tall. He taught motorcycle safety. So naturally he died in a motorcycle accident.

Being a motorcycle safety instructor, he always made sure to wear a helmet, leathers, and his orange reflective vest. None of these things can really protect you from a driver from turning in front of you because their cell phone is more important than paying attention. He dumped his bike and showed very little external injury.

He later died of massive internal bleeding.

A week or so later, one of my best friends and I helped clean out his old room. We were accompanied by our XO. That would be the same XO who within six months would catch shrapnel from a rocket and die of massive internal bleeding. Synchronicity. (That friend was the one I wrote about in a previous section who died of an apparent drug overdose in fall of 2016.)

I didn't give my number before. It was at three when I last came home from war. It has since grown to four and will likely continue to rise. These most recent two weigh on me the most heavily because they were the most preventable.

I can only say for sure that the first of those two has been listed as a suicide. I can't find the official word on the second one, but there were numerous clues in the aftermath of her death. Both of them helped me get home from war alive.

I know their deaths are not my fault, nor are any of the others. Still, we failed those last two. Most of these people will never have their name inscribed on any great momunents,

but they will forever be inscribed on
my heart.

Let's Have Another Round

Content Warning: Blood, War, Death

The previous piece was written summer or fall 2015. It is now spring 2019, and my number is nine. At least I know about nine. I don't keep up with people very well. It could be higher.

They ranged in age from 21 to 52. All but two were younger than me, and all but one of those was younger than I was when I enlisted. Some were friends, and some were people I didn't know very well. But they were all family.

All told, there have been five suicides (three official and two unofficial), two motorcycle accidents, one combat death, and one that was somewhat natural, complications from surgery.

Things I Could Never Tell My Mother

Too   many   already.   And   all
preventable.

Part the Sixth:

Post-Army Life and Career

A Note About This Section

This section will cover some of the places I've worked after the Army (and one both before and after). I have dedicated a good portion of my life to human services and continue to love it to this day. However, as you will read, I have had some pretty terrible experiences, mostly due to corruption, narcissism, and incompetence.

Give Them Shelter

*Content Warning: Sexual Harassment,
Violence*

I spent six months working at a
youth shelter right after leaving the
Army (winter/spring 2013). During my
interview, they told me the programs
were strictly voluntary and that the
facility was strictly no-touch. I had
been wanting to work with at-risk
youth, and not having to restrain was
especially appealing to me. I hate
violence and wanted to work in a place
where everyone could feel safe without
the use of force.

The disillusionment came rather
quickly. Concerns from those of us who
spent the most time working directly
with the youth were routinely
dismissed. Positive drug tests were met
with no consequences, and multiple
clients were clearly selling drugs. One
of them, who had failed at least five

drug tests, was so disruptive that half the staff were preparing to walk out if he wasn't discharged. He left within a week. Another of our drug-dealing clients was eventually discharged after a physical altercation with another client who was higher on the favoritism hierarchy.

Sexual harassment ran rampant at the shelter. One young man was discharged after multiple sexual harassment complaints from both other clients and staff members. The decision to remove him from the shelter was made only after our union threatened a lawsuit.

Another young man was the subject of numerous sexual harassment complaints from female clients. Multiple girls told very similar stories of sexual harassment but were labelled as "not credible", one of whom had worn "inappropriate clothing".

Another girl accused him of punching her in the face. Her complaint was dismissed because she had changed her story. She admitted she initially recanted her accusation after being threatened with retaliation by other clients. She only renewed her allegation after being threatened several more times and beginning to fear for her safety.

All of these girls left the shelter soon after their complaints were denied. He was still there after I left. This also happened to be the young man who was involved with a physical altercation with one of our drug-dealing clients. He was not discharged after that either.

Yet another incident at the shelter still fills me with bitterness. We took in a young man whose parents were no longer able to care for him. It quickly became evident that his needs were far beyond our capabilities.

This young man had suffered such severe abuse as a young child that it was a miracle he survived. His cognitive development had been significantly delayed, and his ability to regulate his emotions was terribly impaired.

One day he had an argument with a young woman. I had followed behind them as it became somewhat heated to try and calm them both down. He charged at her, and I was within inches of having to put my hands on him to protect her.

This was supposed to be a no-touch facility, but there was no way I was going to stand by as this young woman was assaulted. He was discharged that day.

I shook his hand on the way out and wished him luck. I told him I knew he wasn't a bad person but was just very much in the wrong situation. We had failed another youth in the interest of statistics and money.

I don't excuse the behavior of these young men in any way, but I also don't wish to completely demonize them. They all had many fine qualities. They were young men who have been raised in a culture that teaches them to treat women and girls exactly the way they did. They came to us to learn life skills. Part of that should be social skills and how to treat people with respect. We failed them.

Even more so, we failed all of those young women who came to us looking for a safe place. And that is the greatest shame of all.

My last straw came when a young woman I was mentoring was robbed. Clients with jobs had to pay "rent" equal to 60% of their take-home pay which was placed in a savings account and returned to them when they left. Previously, another client's "rent" had disappeared after she gave it to one of my co-workers (who quit soon after). Afterward, "rent" could only be given to certain staff who generally only worked bankers' hours.

One payday my protégé came home with more than $300 for "rent" that she would not be able to pay until the next afternoon. The money was stolen from her purse in her room while she was in a meeting with a staff member. Security footage showed no unauthorized people entering her bedroom during the time the theft could've occurred.

It was obvious who had stolen the money, but almost nothing was done. My protégé was then blamed for her own loss, being told that she should've left her money with the direct care staff, completely contrary to policy (which was designed to prevent theft).

That theft occurred on a Friday morning. I heard about it when I came in for my shift late that afternoon while my protégé was at work. She left the shelter that night. I gave my notice the following Monday.

On my way out, I was written up for not verifying the identity of the person who came to pick her up because she was still a minor. According to my superiors, I had failed to ensure her safety.

(Cue Alanis Morissette.)

Lying Ears

One of the things that helped inspire me to enlist was the years I spent volunteering at a crisis center. I started there in the fall of 2002.

The training program was an intense but rewarding experience. During my time there, I took on a few different leadership positions and made tons of great friends. Having to leave there for the Army was tough.

During my Army days, I would help out with training programs when that calendar and my leaves coincided. No matter how far away I was living, a piece of me was always there. So when I headed back to the Mitten after my Army days ended, it wasn't long before I reactivated at the center and took on yet another leadership position.

Of course, I took on several other things including school and that shelter job during that time. It was hard to keep up, and I was definitely not able to do so at the center. On top of that, I could see that the organization was deteriorating.

Volunteer numbers had been in decline for years. We had been operating 24/7 for over 45 years. I had personally worked a number of shifts on Thanksgiving, Christmas, New Year's, whenever. The one time we had closed was when the building flooded in December, 2003. I took the first shift at our temporary location, waiting about 16 hours for the phone company to switch our service.

When I saw the writing on the wall that 24-hour service was not going to be sustainable, I tried to get people to start making a plan for what we might do. The Borg couldn't have broken that resistance. People seemed all too invested in tradition. Some even said we should shut down completely rather than give up 24-hour operations. I felt increasingly out of place, and in the fall of 2013, about 9 months after my return, I was out again.

A couple years later, I heard that a registered sex offender was going through training. It was an eye-rolling moment but not all that surprising. People often had strange ideas about justice and redemption there.

When an office manager embezzled thousands of dollars, a weeks-long heated debate ensued. Some people were essentially in favor of a cover-up, mostly friends of the embezzler. Several of us, including me, threatened to quit if we didn't prosecute and come clean about what happened.

Ultimately, we did prosecute, sent a letter to donors, and issued a press release. The former office manager received a slap on the wrist.

While I was in the Army, history repeated. Another office manager embezzled an even larger amount of money and had been able to do so undetected for months, maybe years. It cost the organization thousands, not only in the stolen funds but also in IRS penalties.

That second embezzlement was covered up. This office manager did not have friends in the organization. This cover-up was clearly done out of fear of how it would look that they had allowed another embezzlement, one that was much worse than the first one.

So when I heard that the some people in the organization decided to look the other way for a registered sex offender was not that big a shock. I thought it was stupid but probably just a case of a drunken college student taking a piss in the bushes.

It wasn't just one, though, and their crimes were not so light. There were three, all of whom had been convicted of serious sexual assaults, two of them involving minors. A long-time staff member also reportedly confessed there had been several others over the years who had been similarly kept secret.

I met one of these convicted rapists not long before I left. He seemed like a nice guy. I even requested that he be placed in my training group. I was completely unaware of his record, though, and never would have even supported him being invited to join had I known.

Months after I heard about this someone within the organization discovered it accidentally. When he asked organization leaders about it, he was repeatedly told it was none of his business and that the public information he discovered was confidential.

He took one last shot with the board chair who was not among those who had been previously informed. She was not comfortable with having convicted rapists on staff. When she was met with a similar reaction from the leaders who kept this secret, they both resigned.

Soon, the news leaked to partner organizations in the community who encouraged them to update their policies and remove the convicted rapists. They declined. About a month later, it reached the local news media.

When I saw the first reports, I reached out to a few people to encourage them to make the changes that had already been suggested numerous times and to come clean about what happened. They kept refusing for weeks and engaged in a cover-up, trying to convince people that doing background checks was not part of their tradition and that they always accepted people regardless of their past behaviors.

I and others called bull shit. I lost many longtime friends and became persona non grata at the center. Public pressure was intense, though, and legislation was even introduced to require the suggested policy changes. Eventually, they gave in and adopted a background check policy.

Still, that didn't mean things truly changed. A longtime friend of mine took on a consulting role with the organization to help them get their act in order. She quit after a few months. About a year after the initial news broke, the organization was removed from an important community partnership for failing to truly update their practices and be transparent with their operations.

As I write this, the organization is still in operation, but signs indicate the end may be coming. Due to low volunteer numbers, they ceased 24-hour operations in early March 2019.

There is still a whole lot more to the story, much of which is not mine to tell. I hope it is told some day as it could be an important warning tale for other public service organizations on how not to operate.

Home Again

In the fall of 2016 after moving to the Pacific Northwest, I started working at a group home for developmentally disabled adults. During my very first shift, a client shit himself in the middle of the kitchen. Strangely enough, I took that as a sign I was in exactly the right place.

While the job was often challenging, it was not what I would call difficult. After all, there were no boom-booms falling out of the sky, I could go home every night, and I got to feel like I was doing some real good in the world. Towards the end of my tenure there, I was even working on a proposal that would probably keep our core crew in place for 20 years. Unfortunately, come the summer of 2017, things started to decline.

It started with my concerns over potential maltreatment of a client by her family. Management acknowledged the suspicion many of us held that the family often medicated or client in order to manage her behavior. On top of this, she was prescribed some heavy and particularly dangerous medication. We expressed deep concerns, but we were essentially told to be quiet about it.

I chose not to do so. I wrote a letter chocked full of research about the client's condition and the likely deadly consequences of how she was being medicated. That didn't go over well, and someone leaked my letter to a family member who threatened me. (This was illegal in multiple regards.) The bosses said they would fire whoever did it and then did a half-ass investigation, clearly letting people know not to admit anything.

Things were tense, to say the least, for a while after that. They didn't fire me, though. That wouldn't have looked too good considering I had just made it publicly known that I would be filing a mandated report of mistreatment and endangerment. Also, the company soon had some bigger issues to deal with.

Our assistant manager put in her notice after her fiancé broke up with her. He was her supervisor's supervisor. (This may sound odd and unethical, but nepotism and managers dating employees is an everyday occurrence with that organization.)

Finding a replacement for that assistant manager proved to be difficult. Many of us were asked about our interest, including me. We knew better than to take on the job*. There were no applications for months until someone finally applied with absolutely no experience in the field or in management. Of course, he was hired.

We did our best to help this new assistant manager learn his new job, but he didn't take our guidance well. People began to openly insult and disrespect him. While I certainly held a low opinion of him as well, I managed to put on a good act thanks to my military training.

It wasn't long until word began to circulate about him making juvenile sexual jokes. One long-time employee tried to give him advice on being more careful about that. But as I already said, he did not take guidance very well.

One morning in early December 2017, one of my co-workers talked to me about another round of juvenile sexual jokes. She and I were good friends, and everyone on staff knew about her history of sexual abuse and domestic violence. These jokes had been making her uncomfortable for some time, and his latest one was quite personally directed. I encouraged her to report the sexual harassment, and she did.

Later that day she was called into a meeting with him and his two immediate supervisors. He smiled when confronted with some of his behaviors and tried to explain them away. Eventually, he offered an apology along the lines of, "I'm sorry you took it that way." She was sent back to work, not knowing what was coming next but doing her best to finish out her shift.

Several minutes later, the assistant manager who had just admitted to sexually harassing an employee returned, completely alone and unsupervised. My friend said she didn't want to be there anymore, and I was enraged that they did pretty much nothing in response to her compliant. At the very least, they needed to transfer him out. To send him back to work immediately with no supervision was ridiculous.

A few minutes later, he approached her and tried to talk to her. She hunched over in her chair and covered her face with hand, clearly uncomfortable. I walked over and told him, "I suggest you not speak to her." I was very careful with my words (again thanks to that military training).

Despite my intense anger, I was careful not to get too close to him or to raise my voice. I was, however, openly disrespectful as no amount of military training was going to help me hold that back any longer.

After arguing with me for a minute, he invited me to speak with him in his office. I agreed in order to get him away from my friend but turned around when I reached the door. I definitely didn't trust him enough to be alone in a room with him. Right afterward, he left to complain about me to upper management. I haven't seen him since.

When they spoke to me minutes later, I apologized for being disrespectful but let them know this was not a workable situation. They told me they hadn't heard enough yet to fire him. I asked that my friend not be left alone with him. (In later documents, they stated that he was not to work alone with her until she consented.)

They also let me know that we would have an open discussion about our issues with the new assistant manager at our Thursday staff meeting. I was asked specifically to be there as I could be trusted to speak openly.

Things carried on as mostly normal for the next few days. I worked, often completely unsupervised, just like normal. There was no further discussion of our Monday drama. If anything, people seemed to be trying to avoid it.

On Thursday morning, after I had worked mostly alone for hours and just a half hour before that staff meeting was to commence, I was called to a meeting and fired.

Management said I had threatened the assistant manager when I suggested he not speak to my friend whom he had just admitted to sexually harassing. They also said I had created a hostile work environment by coming into work on my off hours when the assistant manager. You may recall I haven't seen him since I suggested he not speak to the person he had just admitted to sexually harassing.

I wrote on social media minutes later that my integrity was worth more than a paycheck. So when this company later offered me several paychecks in exchange for not speaking about why I stopped working there, I refused.

That assistant manager was demoted about six weeks later and fired about six weeks after that. I don't know the reason why. I do know he retaliated against my friend repeatedly after I left and frequently complained about being turned in for sexual harassment. There was also some word that he may have harassed another employee. But a least they kept everyone safe from me.

I'm writing this less than a year and a half after that all occurred. At the beginning, I said I was working on a proposal that could have kept the core crew around for 20 years (not that management would've ever accepted it). The plan probably would've kept people around even if that shitty assistant manager managed to stay, which he clearly would not have been able to do. That core crew is all gone now.

*(One of my old co-workers eventually did take on the assistant manager job after the sexually

harassing one was fired. He quit a few months later.)

My Bridge Over Troubled Water

After the group home fiasco, I landed on my feet pretty quickly. Just over a week later I saw a Craigslist ad for a group facilitator/educator. I had done a ton of group facilitating at the crisis center, and this sounded like a perfect job for me. It was with a domestic violence intervention program, working with perpetrators. That would be quite a change from previous history advocating for survivors, but I welcomed the challenge.

I loved the job and took to it quickly. Within a couple of weeks, I was working mostly on my own. I definitely had some struggles from time to time, but it was an incredibly rewarding experience. I often thought this would be my last job. I certainly wanted it to last until the time came for me to retire.

So what changed? Some of it is hard to write about. I'm still too close to it. For one thing, I was tired. I was doing a long commute once a week that was really getting to me, but all signs pointed to that not going away.

For another thing, I was making a ton of money for the company and being paid painfully little. (A client who used to work in a similar industry once guessed that I was making about twice as much as I was. That would've approached fair.) I also wasn't comfortable with several other things, but much of that will have to wait for some other time.

The biggest part of it was recognizing how much trauma was prevalent in my groups. In particular, I began facilitating a group for women some months before I left. Without exception, they had long histories of trauma and abuse. I had trained to do trauma recovery coaching and put a lot of that into my women's group. I did the same for many of my male participants as well.

When I realized I could better serve the world by focusing on trauma, the dam began to crack. I worked with some great people, and I am incredibly proud of the work I did and many of the participants I had in my groups. Still, the time had come for me to leave that nest.

It was hard. I was very grateful for the opportunity and felt tremendously guilty about bailing out. My boss was clearly upset when I put in my notice. He made an offer for an extremely limited schedule that would allow me to keep my women's group. That was incredibly tempting. The offer did not come with an improvement in compensation, however. While I was certainly not in the job for the money, I couldn't justify staying unless I was going to be paid what I was worth.

Unfortunately, we never had the follow-up conversation. In fact, we barely talked at all my last week or so. He obviously assumed that I was going to take the deal. Instead, I ended up leaving my keys on my desk at the end of my last shift and left with no intention of ever looking back.

I hated that, but I didn't feel like I had a choice. I've also come to realize through this project that guilt has a way of triggering a flight response from me. But that is yet another thing I will mostly save to write about some other time.

Despite the guilt, I definitely don't regret leaving. I am now my own boss and focused entirely on helping people recover from trauma. I won't say for sure this is my last job. It's possible I'll take on another regular job at some point. But I do hope to hang on to this job forever.

Part the Seventh:

Some (Mostly) Happy Things

My Blue-Eyed Girl

Soon after leaving the crisis center (fall 2013) where I had devoted a great deal of time and energy, I was hungry for new volunteer experiences. My then-girlfriend had been volunteering at a cat rescue for several months, and I offered to go along with her one night. I had no idea I'd soon be bringing home the love of my life.

I met her on a Monday, and she didn't have a name. She was only referred to as "Blue-Eyed Baby". She had just come in from an Animal Control shelter. Normally, my ex-girlfriend cleaned the Kitten Room, but extra help earlier in the day shifted duties around. She and I would be cleaning Quarantine that night.

Quarantine was close to full that night, stuffed with quite a collection of sweet, fun felines. One of them kept pawing at me through her cage. She was estimated to be four months old, so tiny and scared. She was a beautiful flame-point Siamese mix. When I took her out to clean her cage, she snuggled up to me for a while and purred. Eventually she climbed up on my shoulders and then bounced around the room a while. It was hard for me to put her back.

After cleaning all the cages, I took her back out for another visit. She was so small that she almost fit entirely in the palm of my hand. I asked about taking her home that night. I was informed that health concerns alone would make that impossible, not to mention the adoption paperwork. The next day I started working on adopting her.

I wrestled with a name for just a little while. With her beautiful blue eyes, I knew I needed to name her after my mother's favorite singer, "Old Blue Eyes" Frank Sinatra. (My mother actually hated cats, so I like to think of this as a joke she would've appreciated.) At first, I considered the name Frankie, but that was too masculine for such a beautiful girl. I soon remembered that Mr. Sinatra's full name was Francis, and so I settled on the female Italian equivalent Francesca.

It took another month before she came home. She had to be spayed and caught an infection at the shelter that required antibiotics. There was also an extra week delay with paperwork issues. Finally, a couple days before Christmas 2013 we made the big trip across town where she would take possession of my house.

A version of this (mostly identical this time) originally appeared on Old School/New School Mom.

I Need a Place to Hide Away

When I first came home from the Army for good, I felt great. I started back at school and was re-connecting with some old social circles. Everything seemed to be going well for me, and I was extremely optimistic.

Changing my address did not change other things, however, as you should've already read. Closing the distance in my relationship didn't make it stronger. It only made the weaknesses much clearer. I already told the tales of how things rose and fell for me at the youth shelter and the crisis center. Everywhere I turned I saw a reminder that I couldn't save the world. My anxiety grew to unbearable levels.

By the fall of that year, I had quit the shelter and the crisis center. I had gone back to school full-time, and that gave me new confidence. I did extremely well in school that year, making the Dean's List both semesters. I had a 4.0 in 25 of the 28 credits I took that year with a single 3.5 in the spring keeping me from perfection.

That spring I had gotten involved with a youth mentoring program through school. By the time the second half of the program began that summer, I was questioning my effectiveness. The youth I was mentoring was a great kid, but he had needs that would never be satisfied by this program. I had no real option but to ride things out until the end of summer semester. I felt trapped and once again guilty for my inability to help someone in need.

By the end of summer 2014, my anxiety was at a boiling point. Being so busy with school and things had given me an excuse to isolate from a lot of my friends. With the end of my relationship, I had pretty well gone into hiding. I started having frequent flashbacks which made me shut down emotionally.

The following summer (2015) I did finally begin to emerge from that hiding ever so slowly. I reached out to some old friends and got back to being at least semi-sociable. The process was difficult with flashbacks and panic attacks pretty much every day. By the time fall officially arrived, though, I was on a good path, and I began to write this memoir.

Well, Actually...

Content Warning: Drugs, Self-Injury

I wrote that last piece in the fall of 2016 and have to laugh now. I was not doing so well. I was in a mixed state with some periods of mania (which is not at all fun). Things were all kinds of up and down for me. I jumped off the wagon (recounted elsewhere). I tried Xanax (which just ended up encouraging me to drink). I started self-injuring for the first time in my life. I was downright crazy and probably should've been hospitalized.

Eventually, I did start to stabilize. In the middle of that rough time, I met a nice lady in an online group (another story recounted elsewhere*). I was beginning to recognize how triggers abounded in my old hometown and that I was stuck in the same rut that had convinced me to leave for the Army all those years before.

I decided it was time for me to go see about this lovely lady. She lived in the Pacific Northwest. So in the spring of 2016 I pulled up stakes and made my way westerly.

You don't get that whole happy story here. For that, you'll have to pick up a copy of Chicken Soup for the Soul: Best Mom Ever!

Who's the Lucky Guy?

Taking the big leap of moving to the Pacific Northwest worked out pretty well. My girlfriend and I ended up moving in together that summer. We created a bit of a furball Brady Bunch with her dog and cat to go with my crazy kitty Francesca, which has sometimes made for some interesting times. (We also took in our neighbor's cat a few years later. Just don't tell the landlord. We were already over our limit.)

About a year later while we were out walking the dog, she told me one of her co-workers asked her when she was getting married. She said, "next summer". I almost asked her who the lucky guy was, but somehow, I was smart enough to refrain. (In my defense, I thought she didn't want to get married.)

Being the smart guy I am, I had her pick out the engagement ring. Putting the thing together and sizing would take about a month. She let me know in the meantime that she expected me to propose. So I came up with a plan. She had spoken several times about watching the sun set on Mary's Peak (not far from our home). That would be the perfect setting.

I had done the hike up to the top a couple of times myself. However, I failed to realize that not everyone in my house walks as much as I do. (I walk a lot. Too much sometimes.) About halfway up the hill she threatened to turn around and ditch me. This happened multiple times. But luckily, we made it to the top.

Then as the sun was setting, with my heart about to explode, I popped the question. "No" was all she said.

I looked around aimlessly. I thought of offering the ring to the dog. A minute later she said yes. I still didn't realize it even at that moment, but I was totally marrying my mother. She would've loved that joke.

And So It Goes...

That's about it for this memoir. I hope you enjoyed reading it. I didn't. That's not me being self-deprecating. I just hate reading my own work.

After reading through things, I also realized that I made the right choice by using mostly stuff I had already written. I couldn't possibly tap into a lot of the emotions I had when first writing these things. I have come a long way from the things I wrote about here and even from where I was when I was writing them.

It was also the right decision for me to do this thing entirely on my own. It would be a lot better with help, but I would never get it done that way. Even on my own, I have tinkered with this thing endlessly and still am far from happy. It reminds me of a line from the late great Townes Van Zandt,

"If it rained an ocean, I'd drink it dry and lay me down dissatisfied."

So it's time to let this be done. I'm glad I did it. I learned many things, much more than I have written about here. Perhaps I will do so in the future, but again, it's time to let this thing be done.

It's not perfect, and I definitely have ups and downs, good days and bad. But so does everyone else I've ever met. In general, though, I'm stable and happy, perhaps more so than I've ever been in my life, all without any pharmaceutical assistance.

I'm strangely grateful for all of these experiences, even though many of them have sucked. They helped make me who I am now. I know my mother would be proud, and that makes it all worth it.

If you or someone you love has been impacted by trauma, I would strongly encourage you to reach out to a trauma recovery coach. It doesn't have to be me. Look for someone you feel comfortable with. There are a lot of great ones out there. And a couple of just good ones. And me.

If you would like to try trauma recovery coaching, send me an email or stop by my website. If you don't like me, I can probably steer you toward one of those great coaches. Or at least one of the good ones.

www.coachdrewsheldon.com

coachdrewsheldon@gmail.com

www.ingramcontent.com/pod-product-compliance
Lightning Source LLC
Chambersburg PA
CBHW021128020426
42331CB00005B/666